Book Review

Reviewed by Philip Van Heusen for Readers' Favorite

Pride is deadly, and it kills happiness. In One Step to Happiness, Ken W. Davies first deals with pride, how to detect it, and how to eradicate it before explaining happiness. The chapter on recognizing pride has an extensive list of questions to help us identify pride within ourselves. Too often, pride hides from us even when we are guilty of being proud. Church splits are often rooted in the sin of pride. The consequences of pride are myriad and destructive. Pride, as seen in Satan, even split heaven, causing a third of the angels to become demons. Contrast all this pride with the humility seen in the life of Jesus. Since Jesus is our extreme example, we need to walk in His humility. Since most people are not humble naturally, we must learn to follow Christ and take on His humility.

After spending most of One Step to Happiness on pride, Ken W. Davies deals with what humility is. Unfortunately, pride is deceptive, and humility is elusive. Too many people tend to be proud of their humility, not realizing that being proud of their humility is still pride. Humility is not about us but about God. Ken wrote, "Humility lives to serve God and give Him pleasure." However, there are many barriers to achieving humility and Ken devotes an entire chapter to them. The proud see all the negative consequences of being humble. Still, the humble understand that the positive relationship with Jesus more than compensates for any hostile reception. There is a significant need for servant-leaders in the church and the world today. I highly recommend reading this book to help you on your journey to happiness and joy, which comes through humility.

Hearing Ken's interview (with Kate Delaney), I can really tell that this book offers SUCH insightful and practical advice regarding why so many of us may be feeling disconnected from ourselves and our happiness.

— Sarah P.

I am looking forward in reading this book, because this book will change my approach to life.

— Julia Cozad

One Step to Happiness

Ken W. Davies

Contents

Acknowledgements

I am very grateful to Ken Proctor and Tony Hodgson for the many improvements they suggested to the text of this book. Thanks, guys.

My thanks also go to my editor, Jennifer Coffey, for the many amendments to the manuscript, to my wife Guinette for her encouragement and helpful comments on the text, and to Martin Fletcher for the title he suggested.

Introduction

It is a common myth that the way to happiness is through fame and fortune. Youngsters dream of becoming pop stars or footballers, while others dream of winning the lottery jackpot. None of these dreams are sure-fire ways to happiness because some of those who have made it to the top have been honest enough to admit that the success has left them feeling quite dissatisfied and empty.

Since we cannot be assured of happiness at the top, it is worthwhile investigating the bottom—and after all, Jesus did say, "Blessed are the meek, for they will inherit the earth" (Matt. 5:5). There is joy and happiness to be had by being humble. Philip Yancey saw this in practice as he interviewed many people, both stars and servants. The latter included many well-qualified people who worked among the homeless, the suffering, and the outcasts. He said, "I would rather spend time amongst the servants than the stars." He went on to say, "They possess depth and richness, and even joy that I have not found elsewhere."[1]

Jesus possessed much joy in his role as a servant of humanity*. If we want that joy, we must emulate his servant heart, discarding our pride. That and humility are two topics which rarely get more than a brief mention in the life of the

---

* See John 15:11 and Luke 22:27

Church, and even then may be poorly understood. I became a Christian in my teens, but even at the age of fifty, I could not have defined or described them well. For the benefit of people in a similar state, I have tried to clarify them so that they can be recognised more easily. We can then see more clearly what effects they each produce.

When a person realises they are proud, it can be like discovering they own a plot of land overgrown with weeds, each a different expression of pride. It has taken a long while for various seeds of pride to take root in our garden, and most of us have not noticed how they were flourishing, nor how deep their roots are. In common with gardening, clearing out these weeds is not just a one-off activity but a matter of frequent attention. Some of us find it difficult to distinguish between weeds and flowers, so this book has been written in the hope that the weeds of pride can be more easily identified and eradicated. The section entitled "Recognising Pride" contains a list of some symptoms by which pride may be recognised and rooted out.

When we consider humility, we discover that it is like a fragrant flower that cannot be bought at a nursery or transplanted from someone else's garden. It needs to be nurtured carefully from seed. Just as weeds inhibit the growth of flowers, so pride inhibits the development of humility. Pride must be rooted out if we want to become humble. My personal efforts at weeding will never be complete, but it seemed worthwhile recording here the lessons I have learned for the benefit of others.

This book focuses on presenting an understanding of both pride and humility so that the reader knows how to discard one and embrace the other in order to gain the joy that accompanies it. The presence of pride or humility can have major consequences in our lives, and some of these are mentioned later in the book. We begin by considering how pride may be associated with spiritual blindness.

The blindness of pride

What initially prompted me to look at the subject of pride was a section in the book called *The Final Quest*². It's a revelation experience that God gave to Rick Joyner. At one point in the experience, Rick was clothed in shining armour, watching Christians battle against a demonic army and winning. An angel near Rick told him to look at some shadowy figures in a small valley nearby. Rick asked if there was some way that he could see these figures better and was given a rather drab cloak. He was told that it was the cloak of humility and that without it, he would not see very well. Once he wore it, he could see these new figures – they were demons of pride, able to attack and weaken the Christians without being seen. With the help of some other demons, they captured the Christians and led them away. At one point, Rick wanted to warn the Christian fighters, but the angel told Rick it would be a waste of time, saying that the fighters wouldn't recognise Rick's authority unless they also wore the cloak of humility.

This incident shows how pride can weaken the Church almost to the point of extinction. It also associates pride with blindness toward spiritual realities, since the warriors who could not see pride were overcome by it. The association of pride and blindness is also found in the Bible.

Biblical association of pride and blindness

The Pharisees were proud, wanting the most important seats and places of honour (Matt. 23:5-7). Jesus called them blind guides, blind fools, and blind men in Matt.23:16-19, commenting on another occasion that their blindness would cause them to fall into a pit (Matt. 15:14).

Whole churches can project an image of pride, and we usually find that it is the prestige and possessions that blind us to our true spiritual condition. An example is the Church at Laodicea, who said, "I am rich; I have acquired wealth and do not need a thing." However, Jesus said, "You do not realise that you are…blind" (Rev. 3:17).

Some New Testament words seem to equate pride and blindness. The Greek word *tuphoo*[3], translated as conceited in 1 Tim. 3:6 means literally "wrapped up in smoke" and used metaphorically to mean "puffed up". The same word is translated *blinded* in 2 Cor. 4:4 where Paul writes, "The god of this age has blinded the minds of unbelievers, so that they cannot see the light of the gospel of the glory of Christ, who is the image of God." No doubt Satan tries to put a smoke-screen around the truth whenever he can.

Because pride and spiritual blindness so often go together, when we find one, we will almost certainly find the other. When they occur together, the blindness of pride can make it self-concealing and thus difficult for an individual to detect in themselves.

Pride as a spiritual disease

In the book of Proverbs we find "The LORD detests all the proud of heart. Be sure of this: They will not go unpunished." (Prov. 16:5) So we know that pride is a sin, but let's for a moment consider it as a sickness—a spiritual one. It is catching, and we so easily infect one another with it. If someone is proud to me, I can be caught out, and be proud in return. Someone may say, for example, that they have just spent two weeks in Australia. I might go one better by saying "Oh, we went there last year for four weeks. We had an absolutely marvellous time." The words of an old song epitomise this approach: "Anything you can do I can do better. No, you can't. Yes, I can." For some people pride is partly inherited— or caught from parents.

The attainments in the world are contaminated with pride: positions of prominence, achievements, possessions, etc. So by having these attainments, we expose ourselves to the infection. Indeed, some people seem to aim for these things in order to be infected. From the prophetic illustration in *The Final Quest*, we can see it is even possible to be infected with pride after a Christian victory.

This sickness is so prevalent that it is largely ignored and generally remains untreated. Even if we know about it and can see the symptoms in others, we often don't diagnose it in ourselves. When we do, it's often not considered sufficiently serious to worry about.

Jesus wanted people to see the riches of the kingdom of heaven and was grieved when they either could not or would not. We can recall that part of Isaiah's commission was to tell people, "Be ever seeing, but never perceiving" (Isa. 6:9). We may have the natural eyesight to view the world around us but lack the ability or desire to perceive certain (or all) spiritual realities.

Paul was well aware of the need for spiritual perception and prays for the Ephesians to see spiritual riches:

> I pray also that the eyes of your heart may be
> enlightened in order that you may know the
> hope to which he has called you, the riches of

his glorious inheritance in the saints, and his incomparably great power for us who believe. (Eph. 1:18-19)

I'm sure that it pleases God if we seek to understand spiritual realities and live in the light of what we have learned.

Vulnerability to pride

At the five-day Royal Ascot event each year, visitors wishing to enter the Royal Enclosure can only do so if they wear formal day dress with a hat or substantial fascinator. The amazing creations that appear on ladies' heads at that event are certainly fascinating, and many must be worn with much pride.

Pride can tempt anyone, but finds people more vulnerable if they have wealth, intellect, or achievements: people who have a good start in life, a big house, expensive car and luxury yacht; those with university degrees; the star footballer in the public eye; and those who enjoy a high position in a business empire, in government, or even a in Christian organisation.

Asaph the psalmist links pride and prosperity when he says,

> For I envied the arrogant when I saw the prosperity of the wicked. They have no struggles; their bodies are healthy and strong. They are free from the burdens common to man; they are not plagued by human ills. Therefore pride is their necklace; they clothe themselves with violence. (Psalm 73:3-6)

The Israelites had been given a warning about prosperity leading to pride before they ever entered the Promised Land. The shortened form of it written below indicates how God's main concern with prosperity is that it so often results in pride. This then drives a wedge between us and God that can grow so large that we do not think of Him, let alone try to please Him by serving others.

> Be careful that you do not forget the LORD
> your God,… Otherwise, when you eat and are
> satisfied, when…all you have is multiplied,
> then your heart will become proud… (Deut.
> 8:11-14)

It is not just the prosperous who are vulnerable. In general, men are more susceptible to pride than women are. They tend to be more competitive and less likely to admit mistakes. If they get lost while driving, they may prefer to 'take the scenic route' rather than stop to ask someone the way. In general women are more ready to ask for directions than men. Men who could benefit from counselling may avoid it because they do not like to admit they need help.

In James 4:6 we read that "God opposes the proud but gives grace to the humble." We find that the Bible records several rulers who became proud and were punished because of it. Uzziah, for example, was proud and was punished with leprosy (2 Chron. 26:16-20), Belshazzar was killed (Dan. 5:1-30), and the king of Assyria lost the effectiveness of his warriors through a wasting disease (Isa. 10:12-16).

Leaders at any level can fall into the trap of ignoring criticism or advice, thereby considering that they know better than anyone else. Sadly, pride has arrived at their door!

Pride makes some people seem shy. This is because these people want to appear strong, so they do not want to reveal their vulnerable side. They are afraid that if people get to know them well, they will also get to know their vulnerabilities, and that would never do. Therefore, they 'keep themselves to themselves', and appear shy.

Some people will not put themselves in 'teachable' positions because that lowers their status and makes them feel vulnerable. Therefore, they miss out on many things that they could learn.

Desire for status

The Roman emperor Justinian built a beautiful church and dedicated it to the glory of God. However, someone claims to have heard him murmur that with this building he had surpassed Solomon.

The desire for status can spur us on to do justice to our talents and encourage excellence. However, we should seek to use our talents well to please God and not to focus on how we are perceived by others. If our status is a major concern, it is normally because our self-perception is so dependent on what others make of us. As Christians, we should know that the only acclaim worth having is that which God can give.

Many people today seem to be insecure—possibly because they have not had good parents or teachers to love and encourage them and provide some form of stability. If people feel insecure, they may well want positions that are thought to carry security—possibly through control of circumstances, people, or money. Unfortunately, people do not always look in the right direction; they should seek the love and companionship of our Heavenly Father for their ultimate security.

Personal insecurity, possibly with low self-esteem or feelings of rejection, can sometimes lead people to compensate through expressions of pride, examples of which are given a few pages ahead. It is thought that there is a direct psychological relationship between insecurity and pride.

It can be tempting to feed our pride by comparing ourselves with others whose ethical standards are lower than ours and congratulate ourselves on being better. We may also consider people who are more successful than us, then try to boost our pride by outclassing them. All this distracts us from serving God and our fellow man. Peter may have wanted to compare his assignment with that of John, but Jesus said, "If I want him to remain alive until I return, what is that to you?" (John 21:23).

In Acts 8 we have the account of a Samaritan called Simon, who had been respected for many years for the sorcery he could perform. However, once Philip came to preach and imparted the Holy Spirit to many people, Simon was no longer a cut above the rest—he had lost his status, and it worried him. He wanted to regain the people's respect, so he offered to pay the apostles for the ability to pass on the Holy Spirit to anyone on whom he laid his hands. However, he was soundly rebuffed for having the wrong motives.

Receiving praise from others

It seems obvious that we should never praise ourselves. As we are told,

> Let another praise you, and not your own
> mouth; someone else, and not your own lips.
> (Prov. 27:2)

So how do we react to praise from others? It seems best to pass this praise to God in one way or another. As Jesus said, "…let your light shine before men, that they may see your good deeds and ***praise your Father*** in heaven" (Matt. 5:16). Below are a few examples of how God gets the praise.

- Jesus said, "I do not accept praise from men" (John 5:41), so when someone addressed him as "good teacher," he drew attention to his Father, saying, "No one is good—except God alone" (Luke 18:18-19).
- The apostle Paul reported the results of a missionary journey, and praise was spontaneous.

  > When we arrived at Jerusalem, the brothers received us warmly. The next day Paul and the rest of us went to see James, and all the elders were present. Paul greeted them and reported in detail what God had done among the Gentiles through his ministry. When they heard this, they praised God. (Acts 21:17-20)

- When Benny Hinn sees the Lord healing people in a service, he readily encourages people to give God the glory for what they see, sometimes by clapping.
- If we are praised, we could accept the praise with a polite "thank you" but praise God in our heart for the talents or abilities He has given us.

Recognising pride

Sometimes we can recognise a proud person easily. They have too great a self-esteem and generally want to have a high status, elevate themselves in some way, or be seen as better than others. To describe pride the New Testament, writers used the word *huperephania*, which means "showing oneself above others." It is translated as arrogance in Mark 7:22. Even today when a craftsman is trying to get a smooth surface, he may call a point "proud" if it sticks above the rest. It's interesting to note that the number of words we have to describe a certain area of life are an indication of how common that subject is, and for pride these are plentiful, e.g. arrogant, disdainful, conceited, bumptious, vain, haughty, and pompous, to name a few. We also have verbs: swagger, show off, swank, and many more.

Pride, however, is not always obvious. In fact some aspects of pride can easily pass unnoticed, leaving us dangerously unaware of its existence. It can be rather like bad breath—you are the last one to know you have it!

So how do we detect it? Below are what could be considered symptoms of pride, which should help us with our detective work. If we recognise pride when it comes, it gives us more opportunity to resist. When we have a disease, we do not see the microbes that have produced it. Similarly, while we may not recognise pride directly, the list of possible symptoms below may help us detect it. I have included many examples in this list because it can be so easy to overlook the fact that they express our pride.

Many sentences have a common start, so this is typed in bold letters and the end in plain text. Bullets have been placed before the second part in sections where the second part may sometimes be more than one line of text. These help the eye to differentiate one ending from another. The reader may like to go thoughtfully through the current list then add more items if they come to mind.

Considering myself better than or superior to the next person or even despising them because

I have: a better car, house, job.
a better education, accent, language skills.
upmarket holidays, clothes, hobbies (e.g. learning to fly).
the latest computer, kitchen gadgets, TV.
a boat, horse, etc.
a better knowledge of the Bible.

I am: slimmer or fitter.
wealthier.
more intelligent.
less arrogant.
less selfish.
more skilled at sports, music, social graces, etc.
a Christian.
stronger (was Goliath proud?).
more cunning and crafty.

I: live in a better area.
can pray more fluently.

Making myself look good or better by:

- belittling other people's ideas, but promoting my own.
- not admitting to mistakes and saying sorry, but possibly justifying my actions with arguments.
- blaming others when things go wrong.
- giving an excuse that sounds better than the real facts.
- telling lies to impress, deceiving, falsifying information, concealing the truth or being economical with it.
- boasting about myself, my family, achievements, possessions, famous people I know.
- doing or showing something to impress, rather than to serve or interest someone else.
- making sure that everyone knows how close I get to the Lord in my spiritual experiences.
- criticising other people, with the implication that I would do things better.
- poking fun at others.
- treating others as though they were children by the way we speak to them (often an unconscious attitude).
- mentioning my great achievements.

Thinking:

- "I'll show them!"
- "My integrity, morality, competence, and understanding will keep me on the straight and narrow. I don't need to check with God much now."
- "God will surely want to fit in with my plans because they are so good."
- "Other people should be around to help and serve me." (presumption)
- "I'm wise, not like some I could mention."
- "They ought to do it my way because I know what's best."

- "There's nothing they can teach me! (I, of course, know it all.)"
- "I'm wiser and more dedicated than other folk; therefore, I should make the decisions and control them." (a minister's admission)
- "I don't think the Bible has got the right idea on some issues. (I know better than God!)"
- "I don't need to go any further in the Christian life because I know it all."
- "I'm quite good at resisting temptation."
- "Our Christian tradition or denomination is better than other people's."
- "You can't have better meetings than the ones we have at our church."
- "Our church practice and theology is better than other denominations."
- "I know I've done the right thing, and I can justify it." (self-righteousness)
- "There's nothing I need to repent of because I'm doing fine."
- "I don't need other people. I am OK as I am and can look after myself."
- "This church/club/society is fortunate to have me as a member!"
- "In general conversation, my words are more important than those of other people, so it makes sense to interrupt them when I have something to say."
- "I can do this job better than anyone else, so no one else should even attempt to do it unless directly under my control."
- "People should look to me for their role model."

Saying:

- "Didn't you know that?"
- "Haven't you been there, done that, seen that?"
    (These can, of course, be said in surprise but also out of pride that wants the recognition that I have known it, done it, seen it, or been there <u>before</u> you.)
- witty or clever remarks at the expense of others.
- anything that is dismissive of other people's efforts or belittles them.
- anything in a patronising or condescending way (without realising that it sounds like that).
- "I told you so!"
- "You're a fool!" (I'm not, of course.)

Wanting:

- status.
- to bolster my ego.
- people to know that I was the first to think of it, say it, or do it. (It is right that credit goes to the right person, especially for patent purposes, but God will ensure that we are rewarded in eternity for the things that matter.)
- to impress people with my home, car, etc.
- to outshine others with my clothes.
- to look good in front of people generally because if one of my weaknesses or flaws gets exposed it embarrasses me immensely and I feel a loss of status.
- to appear more knowledgeable on a subject than is really the case.
- to take all the credit for work to which others have contributed.
- to appear mature or spiritually mature.
- to be considered important (sometimes becoming pompous).

- to be admired for the things I do well.
- to receive recognition from others for my actions or achievements. (People who looked for instant recognition for their deeds received the comment "I tell you the truth, they have received their reward in full" Matt. 6:2.)
- to dominate ("Be shepherds ... not lording it over those entrusted to you." (1 Pet. 5:3)).
- to win every argument and debate, whether I am right or wrong (after all, people should bow to my superior intellect).
- to have the last word on a matter (essentially, win the argument).
- to win every game and contest, whatever the cost, and be recognised as superior (very competitive).
- abilities and public acclaim of prominent people (jealousy, envying other people's ministry).
- fame and glory.
- a good reputation.
- to be respected and honoured, rather like the Pharisees. "Everything they do is for men to see," said Jesus. "They make their phylacteries wide and the tassels on their garments long; they love the place of honour at banquets and the most important seats in the synagogues; they love to be greeted in the marketplaces and to have men call them 'Rabbi'" (Matt. 23:5-7).

Unwilling:

- to accept help when I could do with it.
- to admit lack of knowledge.
- to accept advice from those who may have experience to offer in a given area.

- to acknowledge that my church or organisation is corrupt (typified by Renaissance popes, who were wilfully blind as they plundered the wealth of the Church).
- to show ignorance or lack of understanding by asking a question after a talk. (Did pride stop disciples asking for explanations? Luke 9:45. The Bible says they were afraid to ask for an explanation, and it may be that they feared an apparent loss of face if Jesus chided them for their lack of understanding.)
- to do menial tasks, or anything for which I get no recognition.
- to respect authority or accept it.
- to do anything where I might lose my dignity.
- to try something for fear of looking a fool if I do it wrong or it fails.
- to mix with lesser mortals.
- to let anyone know anything of my weaknesses, so I give the appearance of being totally competent and fine, showing a stiff upper lip, etc.
- to "own up" to having made a mistake or having done something wrong.
- to "confess my sins" to an appropriate person because it would lower my status.
- to praise others for good work or a good attempt.
- to be despised or lose respect.
- to live in obscurity.
- to trust God because I'm not sure that He will do what is best. (I think my way is likely to be better.)
- to acknowledge that my debt is getting out of control.
- to express regret for mistakes or misdemeanours.
- to accept I could be wrong—but blame others or justify my actions instead.
- to laugh at myself.
- to repent.

Enjoying:

- the prestige and power associated with a position, job, or office, rather than the opportunity it provides to serve the people or organisation concerned.
- the downfall of other people.
- correcting others whenever they are wrong.

Ignoring those whom I consider have nothing worthwhile to say to me.

Giving an appearance of modesty or humility. (This may be done with deprecating comments on my own work or achievement when inside I am thinking, "Aren't I wonderful and clever? I hope the other person realises this.")

Sexual pride may produce statements such as:

- "All men are the same. You can never trust a man."
- "Look at what she has just done! Women drivers!"

Racial pride has led to murder and so-called 'ethnic cleansing'. Hitler's attempt to exterminate all Jews is a prime example of this.

Defensiveness can sometimes be a symptom of pride when it is associated with the fear of losing face. There is a security in not having status because there is nothing to lose.

When speaking or writing, the proud person may present thoughts or information that they have gleaned from others, but deliberately hide the fact so that their listeners believe that these thoughts or facts originate from the presenter—thus, they get the credit.

We are often not aware that pride is the motivation behind some thoughts and actions—e.g. when we push into a queue, we unconsciously consider that we are more important than the people we are displacing.

If we criticize God or get angry with Him, we must think we know better than He does, and surely this is pride. If we are angry with Him, surely it is because we think that He should have done what we wanted—i.e. our ways are better than His!

If some new truth or information is brought to the attention of a proud person, he or she may not indicate that it is new to them because to do so would show that they know less than the speaker. For example, an older Christian may not wish to show ignorance of a truth discovered by a younger believer.

The proud may be less willing to learn than the humble because they think they know it all.

Pride may be our greatest challenge

From the list of symptoms above, it is clear that pride can so easily worm its way into many spheres of our thinking. It can be the least conspicuous of all sins, but nevertheless the seedbed from which all other sins grow.

Anyone who relishes a challenge will see that to eradicate pride from our lives is a worthy task indeed. It may even be our greatest challenge.

Possible consequences of pride

I t is instructive to consider the consequences of pride and humility. Firstly, we see that pride can cause disruption and suffering in the following ways:

Pride can cause splits in the Church.

Two Christian pioneers were working well together. Then one of them wanted to take his young cousin with them to help with the work. The other pioneer wouldn't hear of it. As far as he was concerned, this young man was unreliable. They had invited him to join the team before, but he let them down partway through the mission. There was no way he was going to take this youngster on again. Each of these pioneers thought he knew best and that in this instance he was wiser than the other man. Paul might have reasoned in his logical way that since Mark had failed in one mission, he would do so again. Barnabas might have argued from the point of knowing Mark's heart and determination in the present. They disagreed so sharply that their partnership broke up. Barnabas went on a mission with his cousin Mark, while Paul chose a man called Silas to accompany him on his next journey (Acts 15:36-41). Where there could have been a strong team of three people—Paul, Barnabas, and Mark—there were two weaker teams of just two people.

It is a sad fact that sharp disagreements occur in the Church today, leading to splits of one sort or another. Pride plays some part in each instance and continues to spoil the life of the church. How much it must grieve God.

After Peter, James, and John had been privileged to see Jesus transfigured in his glory, they came down from the mountain to find that none of the other nine disciples had been able to cast out a demon from a young man. Whether it was this contrast between the recent experiences of the two groups or not, we don't know, but we find that shortly after these incidents an argument broke out among the disciples as to who was the greatest. Perhaps those with the mountaintop experience thought that they were in some way better than the others. Whatever started it all, the issue of status was clearly one that could provoke an argument—even among the disciples (Mark 9:33-35). This sort of problem was discovered many years earlier by the writer of Proverbs, who said, "Pride only breeds quarrels, but wisdom is found in those who take advice" (Prov. 13:10).

James and John asked Jesus for the best seats in heaven, but their request did not lead to the promise they wanted. They received a lesson on humility instead (Mark 10:35-45). If they had been obeying the command to "Love each other" (John 15:17), they would not have harboured the pride that led to this bickering. As Paul says, "Love is patient, love is kind. It does not envy, it does not boast, it is not proud" (1 Cor. 13:4).

Some of the divisions in churches today are due to the same issue of one person wanting a higher status than another. We can surmise that pride can even cause a split in heaven itself because the passage below is usually understood to refer to Satan, and it's clear he was ejected from there.

> How you have fallen from heaven, O morning
> star, son of the dawn!
> You have been cast down to the earth, you
> who once laid low the nations! You said in
> your heart, 'I will ascend to heaven; I will
> raise my throne above the stars of God; I will
> sit enthroned on the mount of assembly, on
> the utmost heights of the sacred mountain.
> I will ascend above the tops of the clouds; I
> will make myself like the Most High.' But
> you are brought down to the grave, to the
> depths of the pit. (Isa. 14:12-15)

Pride can strain or break relationships.

Where there is a relationship problem, pride is invariably at
the root of it. It may be a case of "My way is best and we
should implement it", "I'm not going to do just what you
want", a refusal to say sorry, or some other expression of pride.

It seems obvious that if you consider yourself better
than the next guy you won't think his ideas are as good as
yours, you won't treat him as equal or consider that he is
worthy of much attention, and your relationship gets little
chance to blossom.

Pride can bring rebellion and lawlessness.

Rebellion and lawlessness can occur where pride wants its
own way. Paul knew that a sad day would come when this
would even be seen in the Church. He said,

> Don't let anyone deceive you in any way, for
> that day will not come until the rebellion
> occurs and the man of lawlessness is revealed,

the man doomed to destruction. He will oppose and will exalt himself over everything that is called God or is worshipped, so that he sets himself up in God's temple, proclaiming himself to be God. (2 Thess. 2:3-4)

This could apply in part to the situation where a church leader tells the congregation to do or believe what he says, rather than what God has made clear in the Bible.

Where the proud person does not rebel openly, he may do so inwardly in bitterness or anger. These feelings can arise, for example, if someone else is given the recognition you think you deserve, or, alternatively, they are not demoted or punished sufficiently for their actions which you dislike. Such a person needs to heed what Jesus said on the subjects of anger and forgiveness in the verses below:

"You have heard that it was said to the people long ago, 'Do not murder, and anyone who murders will be subject to judgment.' But I tell you that anyone who is angry with his brother will be subject to judgment. Again, anyone who says to his brother, 'Raca,' is answerable to the Sanhedrin. But anyone who says, 'You fool!' will be in danger of the fire of hell." (Matt. 5:21-22)

But if you do not forgive men their sins, your Father will not forgive your sins. (Matt. 6:15)

Pride can lead to deceit.

If someone wants to impress others, it is easy to fall into the trap of exaggerating achievements, position, knowledge, or possessions. Sometimes this may happen because we romanticise events, but other aspects are just deceit. This leads on to the next point.

Pride can produce hypocrites.

We may try to be seen as good even if we aren't. Jesus told the story of a man with a plank in his eye who proudly thought he could see sufficiently well to remove a speck from someone else's (Matt. 7:3-5). Jesus called the man with the plank a hypocrite because, by offering to remove a speck from another man's eye, he implied he could see well, whereas the plank would have made it impossible.

In the time of Jesus, some people liked to project a virtuous image by ensuring that they were seen when they prayed. Jesus warned his disciples not to copy their hypocrisy (Matt. 6:5). He also told a story of a servant who abused his position and ends up "with the hypocrites, where there will be weeping and gnashing of teeth" (Matt. 24:50). This is speaking clearly of hell, as described in Matt. 13:50 and several other passages, so we must guard ourselves carefully against this.

Let us remember that Jesus warned the disciples against the yeast of the Pharisees, which he identified as hypocrisy (Luke 12:1). No doubt he used the illustration of yeast because it puffs up bread, just as pride puffs up a person's ego.

Pride can make us more susceptible to temptation.

Those who congratulate themselves on their self-control are more likely to allow themselves to come too close to temptation and then succumb to it. For example, a happily married minister may think he is safe to counsel women alone. However, a grateful lady may express her thanks with an enthusiastic hug on more than one occasion, sparking off unexpected emotions that lead to infidelity and adultery.

The solution is to have a realistic awareness of our will-power and avoid situations where temptations can thrive.

Pride leads to self-reliance and can precipitate a fall.

People in charge of the *Titanic* were proud of their ship and considered it unsinkable. We all know what tragedy that led to, illustrating vividly the text from Proverbs 16:18, "Pride goes before destruction, a haughty spirit before a fall." The *Titanic* incident illustrates how pride can lead to overconfidence and a false sense of security. It can make us oblivious to pitfalls, and we may think we are on firm ground, only to find it opening up beneath us.

Pride may lead to animosity, jealousy, and rejection if others appear to be more blessed.

If someone can do a task better than us, particularly if they have less responsibility than we do, our own pride can become wounded. We can be jealous of them, and may 'hit out' at them in some way, possibly aiming to belittle them if we can. Suppose a worship leader invites a newcomer to enter the group. He may find the newcomer is a highly gifted musician, and the group may respect him more than the original group leader. A proud leader can be jealous of the newcomer's gifts and abilities. He may therefore allocate him only a small part to play or even remove him from the group.

Pride distances us from God.

The psalms tell us, "…whoever has haughty eyes and a proud heart, him will I not endure" (Psalm 101:5). "Though the

LORD is on high, he looks upon the lowly, but the proud he knows from afar" (Psalm 138:6). Being at a distance from God suggests less intimacy. If He "knows us from afar." it presumably means that the Holy Spirit has less influence within us. Do we want to be filled with pride or the Holy Spirit?

Pride can prevent people from becoming disciples.

My wife was a district nurse and injured her back severely one day when assisting a lady to lift her husband at home. A surgical operation helped at one stage, but then her condition deteriorated into yet more pain. In 1996 she received prayer and was dramatically healed. When I recounted her healing to work colleagues, many of whom were scientists, they did not want to believe me. Pride in their own understanding of how things happen, gained through studying for PhDs, etc., was a major obstacle to belief in God.

Jesus commented that pride was an obstacle to belief, saying,

> 'How can you believe if you accept praise from one another, yet make no effort to obtain the praise that comes from the only God?' (John 5:44)

Pride is an obstacle to repentance.

This is because people do not want to admit they have "got it wrong" or acted wrongly. Humility is needed both for repentance and revival. The psalmist said, "In his pride the wicked does not seek him; in all his thoughts there is no room for God" (Psalm 10:4). It has also prevented believers' confession of their faith:

Yet at the same time many even among the leaders believed in him. But because of the Pharisees they would not confess their faith for fear they would be put out of the synagogue; for they loved praise from men more than praise from God. (John 12:42-43)

Pride impedes progress.

Anyone who thinks they know it all won't see the need to listen to the ideas of others. They have an inbuilt barrier to spiritual growth and can become quite complacent. Some people do not become Christians because when they hear the Christian message they think that their atheistic philosophy and understanding is superior. I believe that God is unlikely to give a powerful ministry like healing to proud people because it will just make them worse. Paul said, "If anyone teaches false doctrines and does not agree to the sound instruction of our Lord Jesus Christ and to godly teaching, he is conceited and understands nothing" (1 Tim. 6:3-4).

The people at Nazareth thought they knew better than the Son of God and did not believe what he preached (Mark 6:4f). Because of this, they missed the opportunity to be healed.

Pride counteracts prayer.

Jesus said, "If you remain in me and my words remain in you, ask whatever you wish, and it will be given you" (John 15:7). If we are proud, we cannot possibly remain in a humble Lord and so have whatever we wish. We also read that "God opposes the proud, but gives grace to the humble" (James 4:6), so if we are proud we are opposing Him, and there seems even less chance of God granting our requests. Let us remember the parable:

> "Two men went up to the temple to pray, one a Pharisee and the other a tax collector. The Pharisee stood up and prayed about himself: 'God, I thank you that I am not like other men—robbers, evildoers, adulterers—or even like this tax collector. I fast twice a week and give a tenth of all I get.'
>
> "But the tax collector stood at a distance. He would not even look up to heaven, but beat his breast and said, 'God, have mercy on me, a sinner.'
>
> "I tell you that this man, rather than the other, went home justified before God. For everyone who exalts himself will be humbled, and he who humbles himself will be exalted." (Luke 18:10-14)

We can see from this story how God welcomes the prayer of a humble man so much more than that of the proud. We may not recognise the problem so easily, however, because it is more common for us to express our pride in other ways.

Pride may lead to domination or control.

The desire to be on top, to win at all costs, can produce quite aggressive and evil behaviour. Any form of oppression, including spiritual abuse (control, manipulation, and domination), is not the expression of a servant heart, since the oppressor is not serving someone but demanding that they serve him/her in some way.

It is possible to manipulate situations without appearing to be the main player in the drama. Jezebel was an Old Testament character who enjoyed exercising this form of influence, and the demonic spirit that encourages this type of manipulation has been given her name. The Jezebel spirit is proud and believes her dealings are unobserved. Isaiah wrote of such a being, saying,

> "You have trusted in your wickedness and have said, 'No one sees me.' Your wisdom and knowledge mislead you when you say to yourself, 'I am, and there is none besides me.'" (Isa. 47:10)

A proud person may attempt to lead others but find that some of them are already experienced and well-informed. When this happens, the aspiring leader may feel frustrated because he has lost the chance to teach or disciple them. He may even feel that they constitute competition to his attempts at leadership—competition that could be threatening or difficult to deal with. For this reason, he may try to reject them by attempting to discredit them or exclude them from the group or organisation. In that way the leader can continue unopposed in his chosen role.

The pastor of a church felt called elsewhere, leaving the congregation in the hands of a small team, none of whom had gained leadership experience through their daily employment. As a consequence, they may have felt insecure in their role, and it could explain why one leader singled out a godly and well-educated couple in the church and told them to leave, informing the congregation that this pair were wolves in sheep's clothing. With that couple out of the way, the status of this leader was secure, and she could continue to dominate the church without the risk of being challenged.

Another way that a proud person may try to protect his status is by distancing himself from anyone who he believes is a potential threat. If he says very little about himself, a potential enemy will have very little that could be used as ammunition against him.

Pride may lead to ingratitude.

A proud man may believe that he deserves a lot, and so be less thankful than others for the good that he receives. People who do not give thanks for gifts and presents may also be presuming that it is their right to receive these things, and nothing more is needed.

Pride provokes judgment from God.

- "I will put an end to the arrogance of the haughty and will humble the pride of the ruthless" (Isa. 13:11).
- "The LORD detests all the proud of heart. Be sure of this: They will not go unpunished" (Prov. 16:5).
- Satan is proud and has been hurled out of heaven (Isa. 14:12-15).

Pride can lead to prejudice.

Prejudice is a judgment made without due examination of the facts, and this sort of judgment is often made by the proud who think they know all the relevant facts they ever need to.

Pride can weaken a church or cause stagnation.

If we see much pride in a church, and consider any or all of the consequences above, it will be clear that the progress of that church will be impeded in so many ways that it is likely to stagnate or even go downhill. Awareness of the need to mature as Christians may be replaced by the "We're OK" attitude as in the Laodicean church. In the Revelation church letters, Laodicea was the only church that received no commendation, but was told, "You do not realise that you are wretched, pitiful, poor, blind and naked" (Rev. 3:17). If a church is dysfunctional, it is highly likely that pride will be in evidence there.

Jesus, the model of humility

Not everyone realises that God is a very humble person. In his teaching about Jesus, Paul said,

> Your attitude should be the same as that of Christ Jesus: Who, being in very nature God, did not consider equality with God something to be grasped, but made himself nothing, taking the very nature of a servant, being made in human likeness. And being found in appearance as a man, he humbled himself and became obedient to death—even death on a cross! (Phil. 2:5-8)

Jesus could have chosen to be born in the comfortable home of a noble family. Instead he chose a simple home, becoming the child of Mary, a poor unmarried girl. We can see that the very way Jesus entered this world declared his humility.

The way that Christ lived was an epitome of the suffering servant prophesied by Isaiah (52:13-53:12). There is much that could be said about this passage regarding the things he did for our benefit. For example, he allowed himself to be despised and rejected (53:3) and pierced for our transgressions (53:5), and he bore the sin of many (53:12).

Throughout it all he was humbly obedient to the Father, serving humanity through his sacrificial life and death.

We know that in their pride the Jews wouldn't associate with the Samaritans, but in his humility, Jesus happily spent time with a Samaritan woman, an outcast even among her own people because she was currently living with her sixth man. We see his wisdom because she not only realised he was the Messiah, but also brought other people to believe.

Despite the fact that Jesus was the most powerful person who walked this earth, there were times when Jesus seemed to minimise the miracles he did, such as when he said that Lazarus and Jairus's daughter were just sleeping (John 11:11, Mark 5:39).

Jesus humbly submitted to earthly parents while a child. He paid the temple tax, even though he considered it incongruous for the Son of God to pay taxes to man! He was also submissive to the Sanhedrin, Pilate, and the soldiers, when he could have opted out of the crucifixion at any time. As he said, he could even have called twelve legions of angels to protect him! But his attitude of humility led to authority because we read:

> … he humbled himself and became obedient
> to death—even death on a cross! Therefore
> God exalted him to the highest place and
> gave him the name that is above every name,
> that at the name of Jesus every knee should
> bow. (Phil. 2:8-10)

When we reflect on the humility of Jesus, we often think of the Last Supper. Here we read that Jesus began the meal along with his disciples. Then he suddenly stopped eating, took off his outer clothes, and began to wash the disciples' feet—a menial task done only by servants of the lowest rank.

Yet my Lord did it! Then we read that he carried on with his meal, having taught his disciples a lesson in humility they would never forget (John 13:4). Even after the resurrection, we see Jesus preparing a meal of fish for his disciples on the shore of the lake.

Jesus came to teach people about the kingdom of God and once pointed out the fallacy in reasoning of the people who accused him of casting out demons by Beelzebub. While he defended his teaching, his humility meant that he did not defend himself or his status in any way.

The chief priests accused him of many things. So again Pilate asked him, 'Aren't you going to answer? See how many things they are accusing you of.' But Jesus still made no reply, and Pilate was amazed. (Mark 15:3-5)

Just in case they hadn't realised it, Jesus actually told his disciples he was humble in an invitation familiar to many of us:

> 'Come to me, all you who are weary and burdened, and I will give you rest. Take my yoke upon you and learn from me, for I am gentle and humble in heart, and you will find rest for your souls.' (Matt. 11:28f)

We are well aware of how we respond to Christ's call and come to him. However, we do not always recognise when he approaches us. He may speak to us through the lips of either friend or foe without first announcing himself. For our part, we need to humbly listen to others, not least because it may be through them that the Lord wants to speak. Otherwise, we could ignore or even reject him without realising it.

Because he was a disciple, Peter would have been learning from Jesus. He hadn't learned to eliminate pride from his life, however, because it sometimes stopped him accepting the truth from Jesus. We remember that at the Last Supper,

Peter said, "Even if all fall away on account of you, I never will" (Matt. 26:33). He was blind to his own weaknesses, and Jesus told him, "I tell you the truth, this very night before the cock crows, you will disown me three times." A proud person is most unlikely to accept the truth from someone humble. Peter's response illustrated this when he declared, "'Even if I have to die with you, I will never disown you.' And all the other disciples said the same" (Matt. 26:35).

The Scribes and Pharisees found it easy to reject Jesus. If God speaks to you or me today, we should be aware that it would be in such a way that we can easily ignore or reject Him. God does not normally push Himself to the fore. In fact, most of His activities are behind the scenes and do not appear in newspaper headlines.

Our humility

Many a healing ministry has grown from a burning desire to help others, either physically or spiritually. Even if our humble deeds do not have a physically healing effect, they may well have a healing effect upon relationships, and for that reason it is often easier to work with humble folk than with proud ones.

Kathryn Kuhlman, the evangelist with a powerful healing ministry, said she did not believe there was a harder lesson to learn than that of humility. St. Augustine, an early Church leader, considered it by far the most important Christian grace. Without it, we cannot come close to God, we will not see true Church unity, nor will revival flourish. We should therefore understand what true humility means and recognise any obstacle to this in our lives. Let us consider some aspects.

Status

God could have asked everyone to aim high in order to get some prize. If that had happened, there would be people elbowing their way up the ladder and possibly scratching each other's eyes out in order to get to the top. Very few would get there. Instead, He asks us to aim low—not quite so appealing, but it is something everyone can achieve. Jesus said, "The greatest among you will be your servant. For whoever exalts himself will be humbled, and whoever humbles himself will be exalted" (Matt. 23:11-12). It is good to aim for a high place in heaven, but the journey to the best heavenly seats is via humility on earth.

Jesus wanted an illustration of humility for his disciples, so he picked on a suitable child and said, "Whoever humbles himself like this child is the greatest in the kingdom of heaven" (Matt. 18:4). If we are not naturally humble, it needs a conscious act of will to achieve it.

Many people are familiar with the following statement of Jesus where he tells us of his humility and instructs us to learn from him.

> 'Take my yoke upon you and learn from me,
> for I am gentle and humble in heart, and you
> will find rest for your souls.' (Matt. 11:29)

It's helpful to understand what Biblical writers mean by "humble" in this sentence and others. The Greek word used is *tapeinos*, whose literal meaning is "low-lying" and could be used to describe low-lying ground, as on a plain. We do not generally use words like mountaintop or plain when we refer to people's position today. Instead we talk about "status." In today's society, people acquire status through their achievements in sports, business, politics, etc. Even delinquents want status among their peers and may achieve this by bolder antisocial acts or gang warfare.

For anyone to act humbly they need to ignore any status from their background or achievements and act as though they had none. We see Jesus ignoring his heavenly position as Sovereign of the Universe and acting as though he had no status at all.

We may hear that someone is being 'taken down a peg' or 'put in their place'. We should be grateful that this cannot happen to us if we are humble because we are already at the lowest point. We are most secure when we have nothing to lose—to be at peace if we are not praised and at peace if we are blamed or despised. Humility provides that security.

Humility involves ignoring whatever status we have in life and seeking to meet the needs of others. We can only minister effectively for the Lord if we are not looking at ourselves, but looking to Him and listening for His daily guidance.

Servanthood

The acts of humility are not those broadcast through a megaphone but those done in secret. By serving others, we die to self that we may bring forth fruit. We rarely meet any competition for more menial tasks, so barriers to servanthood are few.

Humility was seen from a surprising quarter in the Gospels—the centurion who asked Jesus to heal his servant (Luke 7:1-10). This centurion had a servant heart because he had built a synagogue for the Jews. Moreover, he not only stooped to ask a favour of a man in the country that the Romans governed but recognised his real position with Jesus saying, "I do not deserve to have you come under my roof." Jesus commended him highly for his faith and granted his request.

Humility is sometimes seen as a sign of weakness – but that is a lie the enemy wants us to believe. It is easier to be humble if we are weak, but much more difficult if we are wealthy or gifted in strength of body or mind. Those who are wise adopt an attitude of humility toward God and their fellow man.

Who is wise and understanding among you? Let him show it by his good life, by deeds done in the humility that comes from wisdom. (James 3:13)

Humility lives to serve God and give Him pleasure. It is not therefore destabilized by tribulation, criticism, praise, rejection, or the accusations of men. If we desire humility, we need to discipline ourselves to serve others rather than elevate ourselves. (See later for some suggestions to humility.) It has been said that when we do not learn how to be humble from our friends, we will learn through trials from our enemies, and it will be a painful experience! We do well, therefore, to learn as much as possible from friends.

Readiness to learn

Jesus tells us to "learn from me for I am gentle and humble." The attitude of discipleship involves a readiness to learn from what we both hear and see. Good sight and hearing go together, for we read, "blessed are your eyes because they see, and your ears because they hear" (Matt. 13:16). This is a contrast to the words Jesus quotes from Isaiah describing those who ignore God: "You will be ever hearing but never understanding; you will be ever seeing but never perceiving" (Matt. 13:14). The latter quotation can sometimes be puzzling. However, when we realise that the "hearing" and "seeing" refer to physical abilities, but the "understanding" and "perceiving" refer to our grasp of spiritual truths, it should make sense. Most people have the ability to see and hear, yet are sometimes unaware of spiritual truths and realities.

Humility and gentleness

When Jesus asks us to take his yoke and find rest for our souls, he links humility and gentleness in the same sentence. This link is not a chance occurrence. If a humble man felt the need to point out a sin in the life of his brother, he would want to do so in the most acceptable way, and this is normally achieved with a gentle rebuke.

The apostle Paul noted the need for gentleness where restoration was needed when he said, "Brothers, if someone is caught in a sin, you who are spiritual should restore him gently" (Gal. 6:1).

Does humility bring us closer to God?

I believe it takes us closer than we would otherwise have been, since Isaiah tells us that God lives with the lowly.

> 'I live in a high and holy place, but also with him who is contrite and lowly in spirit, to revive the spirit of the lowly and to revive the heart of the contrite.' (Isa. 57:15)

In contrast, pride distances us from Him.

> Though the LORD is on high, he looks upon the lowly, but the proud he knows from afar. (Psalm 138:6)

We must be humble and recognize that we not only need God, but that we need each other, both fellow believers and unbelievers. We can even learn from our enemies.

> But God chose the foolish things of the world to shame the wise; God chose the weak things of the world to shame the strong. He

chose the lowly things of this world and the despised things—and the things that are not—to nullify the things that are, so that no one may boast before him. (1 Cor. 1:27-29)

We are commanded to love both God and our neighbour (Matt. 22:37-39), and if we desire humility, we must express it in our relationship to both God and man by giving each of them the respect and honour they deserve. When we truly worship God and focus on how wonderful He is, it must help us to realise how lowly we are in comparison.

Christian confidence

Being humble does not mean that we should adopt an attitude of timidity, rejection, or hopelessness, because we have much to be confident about. Paul tells Timothy that "God did not give us a spirit of timidity, but a spirit of power, of love and of self-discipline" (2 Tim. 1:7). Below are just a few scriptural snippets that give us confidence to hold our heads up high:

- He who began a good work in you will carry it on to completion (Phil. 1:6).
- We may approach God with freedom and confidence (Eph. 3:12).
- Neither height nor depth, nor anything else in all creation will be able to separate us from the love of God (Rom. 8:39).
- In all these things, we are more than conquerors through Him who loved us (Rom. 8:37).

Should we take pride in any aspect of our lives?

Since a human craftsman might take pride in what he creates, it is interesting to see that Genesis states several times that when God had completed a part of the creation there is no mention of pride, but just, "God saw that it was good" (Gen. 1:10b, 1:12b, 1:18b, etc.).

Similarly, an earthly father might take pride in the exploits of a son. However, we find that at the baptism and transfiguration of Jesus, God said,

> 'This is my Son, whom I love; with him I am
> well pleased' (Matt. 3:17, 17:5).

We notice that the word "pride" doesn't appear in these accounts. If we should ever "take pride in" something, we must be careful that we are not elevating ourselves for that aspect of life, but merely taking pleasure in it. It seems to me that we walk on safer spiritual ground if we take "delight" or "pleasure" rather than "pride" in these things.

When considering boasting, we should look at the boasting Paul did—but called himself a fool for doing so. He realised that it was not good, but did so out of concern for the Corinthian church.

> I repeat: Let no one take me for a fool. But if
> you do, then receive me just as you would a
> fool, so that I may do a little boasting. In this
> self-confident boasting I am not talking as the
> Lord would, but as a fool. (2 Cor. 11:16-17)

If we are praised for anything, it can sometimes be helpful for our humility to say how grateful we are to God for the talents He has given us. Some boasting is allowed, and God is pleased if we boast about Him—or our weaknesses.

This is what the LORD says: 'Let not the wise man boast of his wisdom or the strong man boast of his strength or the rich man boast of his riches, but let him who boasts boast about this: that he understands and knows me, that I am the LORD, who exercises kindness, justice and righteousness on earth, for in these I delight,' declares the LORD. (Jer. 9:23-24)

Therefore I will boast all the more gladly about my weaknesses, so that Christ's power may rest on me. (2 Cor. 12:9)

Submission

Submitting to others might be considered a weak and foolish act, but it is an essential element of humility. We recognise God as the supreme authority in our lives, but we must remember that He has placed other authorities there also—authorities such as governments, our boss, our pastor, etc. It might help us to meditate on the fact that Jesus himself submitted to the authorities of his day, including his earthly parents. If we resist submission, could it be that we love ourselves too much?

1. Submission to God

When facing any authority, we have the choice to obey or rebel. We should be obeying heavenly authority out of love. As Jesus said, "If you love me, you will obey what I command" (John 14:15). Willing obedience pleases God and shows an attitude of submission. Obedience that is forced or given grudgingly displays no such attitude.

I don't have a horse, but I understand that if I were given a wild one, I would need to train it or 'break it in' before it would readily do whatever I wanted. If it refused to be broken in, it would be of no use to me and might as well be set free to live in the wild. Any horse that would willingly obey his owner could benefit from the care and protection which that owner will provide. In an even better way, if we willingly submit to God, we benefit from His protection and so much more. We are told, "God disciplines us for our good, that we may share in his holiness" (Heb. 12:10).

Some people can testify that when they have been disobedient toward God they have experienced a reduction in His protection until they have come to their senses.

Jesus made it clear that obedience to the will of God is paramount, saying, "Not everyone who says to me, 'Lord, Lord,' will enter the kingdom of heaven, but only he who does the will of my Father who is in heaven" (Matt. 7:21). If we rebel against God and do whatever we want instead, we may not realize it, but Satan is delighted. It's just what he wants!

It seems obvious that if we want to be resident in Christ's kingdom, we must obey the King. If we think otherwise, we are fooling ourselves. As James says, "Do not merely **listen** to the word, and so deceive yourselves. **Do** what it says" (James 1:22).

2. Submission to worldly authorities

Peter lived in a time when the king was harsh and believers suffered bitter persecution under his rule. Nevertheless, he tells his readers that even if it means they suffer unfair treatment, they must obey authorities for the sake of being obedient to God.

> Submit yourselves for the Lord's sake to every authority instituted among men: whether to the king, as the supreme authority, or to governors, who are sent by him to punish those who do wrong and to commend those who do right…Show proper respect

> to everyone: Love the brotherhood of
> believers, fear God, honour the king. Slaves,
> submit yourselves to your masters with all
> respect, not only to those who are good and
> considerate, but also to those who are harsh.
> For it is commendable if a man bears up
> under the pain of unjust suffering because he
> is conscious of God. (1 Pet. 2:13-14, 17-19)

Just in case we are tempted to think that Peter's view-point is an isolated fabrication of his own, we find Paul giving the same instruction to his readers.

> Everyone must submit himself to the governing author-ities, for there is no authority except that which God has established. The authorities that exist have been established by God. Consequently, he who rebels against the authority is rebelling against what God has instituted, and those who do so will bring judgment on themselves. (Rom. 13:1-2)

Watchman Nee was a person who helped establish many churches in China. He was imprisoned for his faith, but he still urged respect for authorities. Christian persecution continues in China today. The Christians do not pray against the government, but pray that regardless of the circumstances their own actions will be pleasing to God.

The only time when we can ignore authority is when the actions they require of us are against God's revealed will, such as when the disciples preached the gospel against the commands of the Sanhedrin (Acts 4:18-20). We are not only told to obey the authorities that are in place, but to pray for them as well.

> I urge, then, first of all, that requests, prayers,
> intercession and thanksgiving be made for
> everyone—for kings and all those in authority,

that we may live peaceful and quiet lives in all godliness and holiness. This is good, and pleases God our Saviour. (1 Tim. 2:1-3)

If authorities ever treat us badly, Peter makes it clear that we must not react in kind.

Do not repay evil with evil or insult with insult, but with blessing, because to this you were called so that you may inherit a blessing…It is better, if it is God's will, to suffer for doing good than for doing evil. (1 Pet. 3:9, 17)

Peter wrote so that we could be prepared to suffer unfairly at the hands of authorities, if necessary. He makes it clear that we actually benefit from being treated badly providing we react in the right way. His words remind us that Jesus said, "But I tell you: Love your enemies and pray for those who persecute you" (Matt. 5:44). It follows that if anyone in authority appears to be persecuting us, we should pray for them.

Martin Luther King Jr. was a Christian minister, concerned that the black people in America were treated by law as second-class citizens. He took the view that we were all equal in the sight of God and should therefore have equal rights. He encouraged peaceful demonstrations, and when they were met with police violence, his followers were instructed not to retaliate in kind. They were essentially submitting to authority while saying at the same time that the laws needed to be changed. It took many years, but the outcome of this movement was that black and white citizens of America now have equal rights.

3. Submission at work

In the workplace, our boss, employer, line manager, etc. has authority over us in a way that is similar to that of a slave master in New Testament times. Paul wrote, "All who are under the yoke of slavery should consider their masters worthy of full respect, so that God's name and our teaching may not be slandered" (1 Tim. 6:1). We may be able to discuss issues with our boss, but ultimately we need to submit to his or her decision, and they should find such an attitude pleasing and worthy of respect.

4. Submission in church

We have already seen that Paul told his readers, "There is no authority except that which God has established." The Lord sends us leaders, and Jesus makes it clear that we should accept them, saying,

> 'I tell you the truth, whoever accepts anyone
> I send accepts me; and whoever accepts me
> accepts the one who sent me.' (John 13:20)

The leaders we have are there to be obeyed, even if they are imperfect and fallible like the rest of us. In the book of Hebrews we are told:

> Obey your leaders and submit to their authority. They keep watch over you as men who must give an account. Obey them so that their work will be a joy, not a burden, for that would be of no advantage to you. (Heb. 13:17)

Paul is concerned that those who lead the Church have quite a responsibility and are thus to be given due respect. He writes:

> The elders who direct the affairs of the church well are worthy of double honour, especially those whose work is preaching and teaching. (1 Tim. 5:17)

Even if we doubt the wisdom of those in authority, we are nevertheless told to obey them.

A new minister in one church sought to introduce new ideas, but was severely hampered by continued criticism over many years from a vocal group of older members. It was only God's anointing and the minister's perseverance that initially kept the church from closure, and finally caused it to flourish. How much better would it have been if all the members had supported the minister wholeheartedly from the start!

Since none of us are perfect, it is not surprising that leaders are also imperfect. However, when Jesus was on earth he still said they should be obeyed.

> Then Jesus said to the crowds and to his disciples: 'The teachers of the law and the Pharisees sit in Moses' seat. So you must obey them and do everything they tell you. But do not do what they do, for they do not practise what they preach.' (Matt. 23:1-3)

Jesus is telling the Jews to obey even corrupt leaders who didn't practice what they preached! Obedience can bring blessing, as we see in the case of Naaman (2 Kings 5).

Naaman had leprosy and came to Elisha the prophet for healing. When he was told to wash in the river Jordan seven times, he was angry and very nearly didn't do it.

Perhaps it seemed undignified. If he really had to wash in a river, he reckoned that Abana and Pharpar, the rivers of his native Damascus, were better than the Jordan. Fortunately for Naaman, his servants persuaded him to follow Elisha's instructions because by so doing he was healed. In this account we see how God blessed Naaman when he eventually submitted and followed orders. From an incident in the life of King Saul, however, we see the consequences of disobedience.

On one occasion, Samuel gave King Saul a command that the king decided to interpret in a way that suited himself and not how God intended. As a result, Samuel had to admonish Saul, who forfeited his kingdom as a result. The full story is in 1 Sam. 15:1-23. As it happens, we benefit from Saul's actions because it led to the following pronouncement from Samuel:

> 'Does the LORD delight in burnt offerings
> and sacrifices as much as in obeying the voice
> of the LORD? To obey is better than sacrifice,
> and to heed is better than the fat of rams.
> For rebellion is like the sin of divination, and
> arrogance like the evil of idolatry.' (1 Sam.
> 15:22-23)

If ever we contemplate rebellion, we should be sobered by the thought that we could be practising witchcraft!

5. Faith and Submission

Faith is intimately connected to submission. We can see this on two accounts. Firstly, if we have faith and truly trust in God, we will do whatever He asks, even if it seems hard, difficult, or even stupid to the human mind. We will love and forgive, for example, even when we don't feel like it. In this way our faith leads to submission. Similarly, when we submit to authority in difficult or harsh circumstances, we demonstrate the level of our trust in God's command about obeying authorities.

Believers with great faith will recognise and respect the authorities that God gives to man. We see this when even a Gentile centurion gave Jesus respect, saying:

> "For I myself am a man under authority, with soldiers under me. I tell this one, 'Go,' and he goes; and that one, 'Come,' and he comes. I say to my servant, 'Do this,' and he does it." When Jesus heard this, he was astonished and said to those following him, 'I tell you the truth, I have not found anyone in Israel with such great faith.' (Matt. 8:9-10)

It was when Jesus saw how the centurion recognised authority that he knew the man had great faith. Jesus links the subjects of submission and faith on another occasion. When his disciples ask him to increase the faith that they had, he immediately launches into a story about servants dutifully carrying out their master's commands (see Luke 17:5-10).

Lack of Humility

The scriptures make it clear that true faith and submission go together, and since submission is part of humility, faith and humility should be seen together also. Serving God and our fellow man is an important aspect of our Christian life, and the following scripture makes it clear that a life without obedience and service is a life that has no chance of entering heaven.

> "Not everyone who says to me, 'Lord, Lord,' will enter the kingdom of heaven, but only he who does the will of my Father who is in heaven." (Matt. 7:21)

This is not a lone scripture on this subject because when Jesus divides the sheep from the goats in Matt. 25:41-46, he tells those who did not minister to the hungry, thirsty, strangers, prisoners, or ill-clad that they are destined for eternal fire and punishment.

An unwillingness to submit and serve others leaves us short of our intended place in the kingdom. Our problem is often not just a lack of humility but being unable to see how badly we lack it. Psychologists say we have an integrity blind spot, with almost unlimited capacity for self-deception. It is so easy for many of us to deceive ourselves that we are good.

Signs of humility

Because humility is not well understood, it may be helpful to read through the list below, which could be considered signs of humility. I've grouped these roughly under three headings, which I hope will be helpful.

Ignoring status

- Considering ourselves as having no status, so that people's criticisms or contempt will not get us down. It means that we do not have to worry about defending status. Nor do we have to worry about being 'put down' because with no status, you cannot get any lower!
- Not comparing ourselves with others to see who is 'doing best'.
- Not seeking authority, to be in charge, or to be prominent ("the head of the table" as Jesus put it).
- Not being jealous or upset, but pleased when others are promoted, given authority, or honoured in some way, while we stay as we are or even have to give up some role.
- Being obedient to the Lord, and being quite content in the role of a servant.

- Discarding independence and individualism, submitting to authority, and being accountable to others for our actions.
- Considering our own good deeds not worth mentioning. Having complete confidence in the mercy of God rather than our own efforts or intentions.

Appraising self wisely

- Agreeing with the truth, and thinking truthfully about ourselves.
- Having a sane assessment of our gifts and abilities (Rom. 12:3).
- Considering the punishment we deserve rather than the good we have done. Being disgusted with our sins and stupid actions, and repenting of them quickly.
- Not presuming to have complete knowledge, but always ready to learn.
- Recognising when we need help or advice, being ready to seek and accept it when necessary.
- Accepting correction when necessary.
- Not considering ourselves good because of our good works, just obedient! "There is only One who is good. If you want to enter life, obey the commandments" (Matt. 19:17).
- Recognising how weak we are by ourselves and how much we need God: "Apart from me you can do nothing" (John 15:5).
- Being willing to talk about our failures and weaknesses, and letting others see them. The apostle Paul received "a thorn in the flesh" (2 Cor. 12:7) in order to stop him being conceited. When he asked God to take this away, God said, "My grace is sufficient for you, for my power is made perfect in weakness." As a result, Paul declares,

"Therefore I will boast all the more gladly about my weaknesses, so that Christ's power may rest on me" (2 Cor. 12:9).

- Being ready to laugh at ourselves because we have no self-image to maintain.

Serving

- Setting aside self-interest and the things that are rightfully ours in order to serve with our time and resources, including money. Servanthood is not for special occasions, but for life.
- Laying down our lives for others (John 15:13).
- Recognising the gifts and abilities of others, and encouraging their use on appropriate occasions.
- Appreciating just how much other people do for the Lord. We are told, "Honour one another above yourselves" (Rom. 12:10) (e.g. ask prayer from others).
- Having no personal agenda, but doing what pleases God and giving all glory to Him.
- Accepting our responsibilities rather than demanding our rights. We don't have any rights anyway as far as God is concerned because everything we receive from Him is a gift.
- Serving others by using natural or spiritual gifts (e.g. healing) without becoming proud in the process.
- Willing to welcome, greet, serve, or converse with anyone, regardless of their status.
- Willing to do a job without recognition or praise from men. Jesus said, "I do not accept praise from men" (John 5:41). Even when he was called good, he pointed to his Father as the only one who was good (Luke 18:19).

When Jesus healed the sick, his action carried the message that God loved them. Even if we cannot heal, whatever service we give to others contains a message of love that can have more impact than any amount of preaching.

Whatever service we provide for others is also for Jesus (Matt. 25:40) and will be rewarded by him. There are countless ways in which we can serve. Jesus gives examples of feeding the hungry, entertaining a stranger, providing clothing, looking after the sick, prison visiting, and washing feet. A list of scriptural references to serving is given in the appendix. It is interesting that a by-product of serving others is that we gain their trust.

The garment of humility looks drab beside the attractive cloak of pride. Perhaps that is why some of us don't wear it readily. Wendy and Rory Alec, founders of God TV, found what humility was like when they tried to start God TV because they had to be reduced to almost impoverished circumstances before God could use them.

Having learned humility, when Wendy published *Journal of the Unknown Prophet*, she was originally not going to cite herself as the author and claim that all the prophetic words it contained were given to *her*. It was only the argument of friends that persuaded her that it was necessary in order to make herself accountable.

False humility

We are being humble if we bring ourselves low in order to serve God and our fellow man freely, but if we lower ourselves for any other reason, it might resemble humility but would be false. It can actually lead to pride if we continue to focus on ourselves. Remember how Moses began to put himself down at the burning bush by saying, "Who am I, that I should go to Pharaoh and bring the Israelites out of Egypt?" (Ex. 3:11). God became angry when Moses continued in this negative vein. If we think that our failings stop us doing God's will, it may be that unconsciously we think that God cannot overcome them.

Some examples of false humility are:

- belittling ourselves—'putting ourselves down', e.g. saying that we cannot do a job when we really can
- treating our body harshly
- forcing ourselves to observe rules and regulations (Col. 2:23)
- considering ourselves worthless or inferior
- sham confession—adopting an attitude of repentance to look good, but not having a repentant heart

For some people, the mention of humility automatically calls to mind the "so very umble" Uriah Heep of Charles Dickens's fame. That fictional character in *David Copperfield* was a dangerous deceiver and has probably done more to devalue the word humble in popular understanding than anyone else, many subconsciously associating it with a smug, sanctimonious piety. There are Christians like that, mistakenly convinced that they should present the appearance of being timid, submissive, and diffident.

If we lead a life that involves certain religious activities, it can leave us in the state that Paul mentions in his letter to Timothy—that of having a form of godliness but denying its power (2 Tim. 3:5). This sort of life means lowering ourselves to submit our body and mind to the discipline of these activities, but this of itself is not true humility since our submission is to the discipline of the activities and not to God and our fellow man. If we take part in religious activities, it can allow us to think we are good because we do them (pride), but as Paul observed to the Colossians, there is often a false humility associated with these acts.

Barriers to humility

The desire to control is one of the most common barriers to humility. It can also divide and break up churches. Even if we do not try to control from a human standpoint, we may try the route that Martha took with Mary, coming to the Lord and saying, "Tell her to help me!" The disciples came to Jesus and wanted him to stop an outsider casting out demons in Christ's name. He would not bow to this sort of 'prayer' where some of his people wanted to enjoy a privileged position but stop others at work for the kingdom.

Sadly, at one time in Church history, Christian leaders sought to control people by being the sole interpreters of the Bible. Consequently they strongly opposed John Wycliffe translating the scriptures into the language of the people.

Sometimes the motivation behind control is to stop people making errors of judgment. However, we must all be allowed to make some mistakes—it is one of the ways that we learn and part of our God-given free will.

Control prohibits teamwork and servanthood, whatever the motivation. John Bevere has rightly said that Satan cannot stop God giving us gifts, but he can do his best to intimidate us so that we do not use them.

We remember that Jesus warned his disciples of the dangers of authority, saying, "You know that those who are regarded as rulers of the Gentiles lord it over them, and their high officials exercise authority over them. Not so with you. Instead, whoever wants to become great among you must be your servant, and whoever wants to be first must be slave of all. For even the Son of Man did not come to be served, but to serve, and to give his life as a ransom for many" (Mark 10:42-45).

There is a sad story in Numbers 16 where a group of Israelites thought Moses had too much authority and challenged him because they thought they were on a par with him. God showed these people where they stood, quite dramatically—"the ground under them split apart and the earth opened its mouth and swallowed them" (Num. 16:31-32).

Concern for status within the Church or group can lead to a 'platform mentality' where a person wants to be visible at the front of a meeting, preaching, leading worship, teaching, etc. Not only do they want to be visible, but they want to retain these roles. If they stepped aside and allowed others to gain experience, they might lose status if the newcomers eventually outshine and replace the person currently in the prominent position!

Possible consequences
of humility

Be criticised or misunderstood

J esus did not criticise anyone who was trying to serve
him, but unfortunately we can't say the same of all of
his followers.

For example, when a lady used a whole jar of perfume
on Jesus, she got criticised for 'wasting' such an expensive
item. Perhaps it was thought that since a rich young ruler was
told to sell all that he had and give to the poor, everyone else
who had expensive items should do the same.

When Mary took the place of a disciple and sat at the
feet of Jesus, Martha was critical of her sister, believing that
because she felt a responsibility to prepare the meal, Mary
ought to do the same.

Then, on another occasion, one of Jesus's followers was
driving out demons in Jesus's name, and because he wasn't
actually part of the official twelve, the twelve thought he
should not be doing it.

In each of these three instances[1] we see people trying to
serve Jesus in the way they felt was right. Each of them actu-

---

[1]   (Matt. 26:9), (Luke 10:40), (Mark 9:38)

ally received commendation from the Lord, but was criticised by others who thought they knew best. So no one who tries to serve the Lord today should be too surprised if their actions are criticised or misunderstood—even by fellow disciples.

Become rejected

The Sanhedrin was the religious authority and had some civil power in the country. Jesus did not have their worldly authority, but he had divine power, and furthermore, he was serving the people in a way that they could not. Not surprisingly, the Sanhedrin did not like it. In the circumstances, they may well have felt insecure, with their status crumbling away. Their action was to reject him totally from society and fix him to a cross. In our generation we have seen Christians persecuted for their faith by the authoritarian regime of communism. To a lesser extent, Christians in the UK are being persecuted when they express their faith in ways that clash with 'equality' legislation. In many ways we can see that rejection of the humble still goes on. We should not be too surprised at Christian persecution, since Paul wrote, "In fact, everyone who wants to live a godly life in Christ Jesus will be persecuted" (2 Tim. 3:12).

If we are ever in a church or group where we find we have more knowledge or talent than the leader, they may reject us because they fear losing their status amongst their followers. The rejection could take the form of expulsion, unfounded criticism, or forbidding us to take part in an activity where they believe we will excel.

Be despised

Truly humble folk do not boast about the things they are good at or even mention the things they are quietly getting on with. Because of this, they may get overlooked and even despised because they are not mixing with the elite of any group to which they belong.

Extra temptations for those trying to be humble:

Become angry or bitter if we are rejected, despised, criticised, or misunderstood. If we are seen as being at the bottom of the ladder, there are those above who can descend on us from a great height.

Lose some of our servant vision if we are ever given authority, and be tempted to control others. (Saul was given the authority of a king in order to serve his country, but trying to eliminate David, God's chosen replacement, was certainly not a service to Israel!) In his wisdom, God has given us free will, so that we in turn can choose whether or not to obey.

Neglect our personal needs by immersing ourselves in serving others. We all benefit from rest, healthy exercise, and companionship. If we have a dog, we give it all of these things, so we should not deny them to ourselves.

Neglect the greatest commandment

If we lock ourselves too tightly into the role of a servant, we can neglect the most important commandment:

> "'Love the Lord your God with all your heart
> and with all your soul and with all your mind.'
> This is the first and greatest commandment."
> (Matt. 22:37-38)

It can be so easy to focus on ministering to the needs of others that we do not spend quality time with God. To complete a task for a friend or prepare and lead a meeting may give us a sense of achievement that seems more tangible than loving God with everything we have. The pressures to do these and other activities may also seem greater than the need to love God. It is something we must guard against.

Receive rewards:

- **Salvation.** "For the LORD takes delight in his people; he crowns the humble with salvation" (Psalm 149:4).
- **God will live with us.** "I live in a high and holy place, but also with him who is contrite and lowly in spirit, to revive the spirit of the lowly and to revive the heart of the contrite" (Isa. 57:15).
- **God gives us grace.** "He mocks proud mockers but gives grace to the humble" (Prov. 3:34).
- **Understanding and guidance.** "He guides the humble in what is right and teaches them his way" (Psalm 25:9).
- **We receive heaven's esteem and commendation.** "This is the one I esteem: he who is humble and contrite in spirit" (Isa. 66:2). If we are good also, we will hear "Well done, good and faithful servant" (Matt. 25:21).
- **We will receive honour.** We are not promised earthly honours, such as a knighthood or honorary doctorate at a respected university. Instead, we are promised honour in heaven. Jesus said, "My Father will honour the one who serves me" (John 12:26). We could not get honour from anyone better.
- **Our light will shine.** If we serve others instead of critically tearing them down, we will gain recognition that cannot be achieved in any other way. As Isaiah says, "If you do away with … the pointing finger … and if you

spend yourselves on behalf of the hungry and satisfy the needs of the oppressed, then your light will rise in the darkness, and your light will become like the noonday" (Isa. 58:9,10). Mother Teresa spent herself unreservedly to tend the poor in Calcutta and set a standard for servanthood that was unequalled in the twentieth century. Her light shone so brightly that on her death she was given the rare honour of a state funeral in India, even though the country was mainly Hindu and Muslim.

- **We will inherit a wholesome land.** Jesus said, "Blessed are the meek (humble), for they will inherit the earth" (Matt. 5:5) and God had told Solomon, "If my people, who are called by my name, will **humble themselves and pray** and seek my face and turn from their wicked ways, **then will I hear** from heaven and will forgive their sin and will heal their land" (2 Chron. 7:14).

- **Our prayers get a better reception.** We understand this from the word God spoke to Solomon but also see it in other contexts, as when Daniel was told, "Do not be afraid, Daniel. Since the first day that you set your mind to gain understanding and to humble yourself before your God, your words were heard, and I have come in response to them" (Dan. 10:12). Jesus emphasises the point when he tells the story of the Pharisee and the tax collector praying by concluding that the man who asked mercy for his sins was justified because of the humble way he approached God. (Luke 18:10-14).

Jesus also teaches this lesson through his own example, and we learn from the book of Hebrews that his prayers were received well in heaven because of his reverent submission to the Father. The reverence in his attitude shows his natural humility in the way he respects and honours his Father.

> During the days of Jesus' life on earth, he offered up prayers and petitions with loud cries and tears to the one who could save him from death, and he was heard because of his reverent submission. (Heb. 5:7)

As an example of someone who really humbled himself, we have the leper who fell with his face to the ground as he begged for help. We are more ready to humble ourselves if our plight is desperate.

While Jesus was in one of the towns, a man came along who was covered with leprosy. When he saw Jesus, he fell with his face to the ground and begged him, 'Lord, if you are willing, you can make me clean.' Jesus reached out his hand and touched the man. 'I am willing,' he said. 'Be clean!' And immediately the leprosy left him. (Luke 5:12-13)

This account makes me wonder if we adopt such a humble attitude as we should to bring our requests to God. Does pride deter us from prostrating ourselves and begging as we pray? The humility and desperation of the leper evoked compassion in Jesus (Mark 1:41). If we adopted the leper's attitude more often in our prayers, perhaps we would experience more compassionate responses from God.

- **We will receive revelation.** This is an important point for any Christian disciple. Where pride might say "I know all I need," humility will say "I am ready to learn more." God has a way of hiding truth from one person but revealing it to another, as we know from Jesus.

> At that time Jesus said, 'I praise you, Father, Lord of heaven and earth, because you have hidden these things from the wise and learned, and revealed them to little children.

Yes, Father, for this was your good pleasure.'
(Matt. 11:25-26)

The wise and learned would normally have a head start in understanding, but here the reverse is true. Why should our Father discriminate against them? The wise and learned are often proud, but little children are not. So we see that our Father is stacking the odds in favour of the humble. Remember that Jesus said, "Blessed are the poor in spirit, for theirs is the kingdom of heaven." The poor in spirit will often be humble. Thus on two counts we see that the humble are more likely to enter heaven. Humility is associated with a teachable nature and embodies a willingness to learn from anyone who God sends to us.

The parables Jesus told were stories that could be understood in two contexts—the natural world and the spiritual one. Because of this, it was a method of giving information to one group but hiding it from another. He said:

> "The secret of the kingdom of God has been given to you. But to those on the outside everything is said in parables so that, 'they may be ever seeing but never perceiving, and ever hearing but never understanding; otherwise they might turn and be forgiven!'"
> (Mark 4:12)

As with the parables, the concept of sight can be understood in two contexts —natural sight on the one hand and perception of spiritual realities on the other. Those who were humble enough to ask for an understanding of the parables received it. In this way Jesus could preach without casting pearls before pigs! (See Matt. 13:11-17.)

Jesus told us in Matt. 11:29, "Learn from me for I am gentle and humble." We need to learn humility, and who better to teach us than one who is humble? If we learn anything from the proud, we are most likely to learn pride!

If we are humble and seeking God, he may even reveal scientific information to us, as he did to Professor Samuel F. B. Morse, who attributed his invention to inspiration that God gave him. He claimed that when he could not think what to do next, he prayed, and God helped him. Other people have also attributed inventions to divine inspiration.

- **We are more likely to see revival.** The Reformation began in the very unassuming setting of an ancient wooden chapel at Wittenberg, Martin Luther being the preacher. God chose this place for a revival in preference to the thousands of cathedrals and parish churches that were available to him.

The modern Pentecostal revival also began in a simple setting in Azusa Street, Los Angeles, in 1906, where a little prayer group focused on God. The group was led by William Seymour, a plain black man, blind in one eye. It was the dawn of a new age for the Church worldwide. In each of these cases, God had chosen to work outside the established Church because that was largely in the hands of men.

- **It enables unity.** Humility is essential in order to bring unity in the Church. Where leaders recognise humility in one another, they know they can work together.

Let us remember that when the disciples nearly split up over who was the greatest, Jesus said, "If anyone wants to be first, he must be the very last, and a servant of all." The servant heart and the serving action will heal any rift. If James truly serves Peter, and Peter serves James, how can they be anything but united? Remember the prayer of Jesus in John 17, when he prays to the Father for unity between his disciples? We can bless Jesus and help his prayer to be answered. We just need to humble ourselves and serve one another with love.

The apostle Paul puts harmony and humility together when he writes, "Live in harmony with one another. Do not be proud, but be willing to associate with people of low position. Do not be conceited" (Rom. 12:16).

Proud people are more concerned for their own interests than those of others. Therefore the humble are easier to work with.

If we are in a church of humble people, we will be serving one another in love, not competing for prominent places, but ready to serve in areas where we are competent or ready to learn from others. Onlookers should see a fellowship that is both loving and united. Each person should serve God and his neighbour by working at relationships, conscious of commands, such as "Be at peace with one another" (Mark 9:50), "Be devoted to one another in brotherly love" (Rom. 12:10), and many more.

One would expect good teamwork when all team members seek to serve. If teamwork becomes difficult, it could be because one person wants his own way, alternatively expecting or demanding that someone does something he finds stressful. For example, a spontaneous extrovert team leader may expect everyone else to participate in the way that they do, but it could be that quieter individuals who have a more planned approach to life may not be able to comply. We need to have a good understanding of one another to work together well as a team.

Unity commands the respect of the world. We expect a football team to be united in a match. Surely the Church should be the best team the world ever sees.

Pride and humility
in leadership

Reverend Josiah Haskins wrote a sermon titled "Humility" then filed it away. He wanted to save it for a really big occasion when he could impress a lot of people.

When addressing elders in a letter, Peter reminds them that humility is a prerequisite for leadership, saying, "Be shepherds... eager to serve; not lording it over those entrusted to you" (1 Pet. 5:2-3).

Leaders are no more immune to the temptation of pride than the rest of us. In fact they face issues in their leadership roles that others do not. The ones who become good leaders are truly humble people. Let us look at just a few.

King David had the humility to accept correction from one of his subjects after he had committed adultery with Bathsheba (2 Sam. 12:1-13). When we consider David's other activities, we notice that even though David's defeat of Goliath had a major impact at the time, he does not boast about this in any of his psalms.

Prophets are often chosen by God to lead His people—though their leadership may not be part of a structured position. They need to be humble if they are to serve God and man effectively. If they were proud, they would be at a distance from God ("the proud he knows from afar" Psalm 138:6) and thus find it difficult to hear Him clearly, even if He wanted to communicate through them.

We see some of the prophets doing things that were very humbling, such as Isaiah walking around stripped (possibly wearing a loincloth) and barefoot at God's command (Isa. 20:2). Scripture states this very simply, but when someone is asked by God to adopt a socially unacceptable mode of dress, it lowers their social standing, and they may lose influence and the respect of their peers. Rees Howells experienced this when God told him to dress plainly and wear no hat when it was the convention of the day to keep one on outdoors. For Christians, church attendance is not just considered socially acceptable, but spiritually necessary. It is not surprising that Rees was also criticised by fellow Christians when he stopped attending church. They didn't know that God had told Rees to do this so that he could spend more time in prayer and Bible study.

We also see the humility of Isaiah when he encounters God in the temple. "'Woe to me!' I cried. 'I am ruined! For I am a man of unclean lips...'" (Isa. 6:5).

It was only after this declaration that God gave Isaiah the commission to be his representative. Whatever authority we may have, whether natural or supernatural, we must not rejoice because we have it, but follow the example of Jesus who had all authority and used it to meet the needs of those around him.

After the Archbishop of York, Dr. John Sentamu, had married his daughter to her groom, he removed his clerical robes and proceeded to the reception kitchen to cook for the crowd of guests at the large reception—a servant indeed!

Servant leaders:

- lay down their lives for their followers.
- are in leadership to make it possible for the desires, needs, and aspirations of others to be fulfilled, not to fulfil their own desires, needs, and aspirations.
- encourage subordinates, and devolve responsibility to them if they are capable of taking it.
- act like a coach in the development of others.
- create an environment where others can flourish and reach their potential.
- do not hold on to authority, but can let it go with ease.
- rejoice when others excel.
- say, "Stand on my shoulders, go beyond where I have led you."
- are not interested in the status or trappings of authority.
- see a bigger picture than just their own involvement and can stand back, letting others take over in order for that picture to be achieved.
- are constantly learning; they look for and take advice from others.
- know who they are in God, having a sound assessment of their abilities.
- make themselves accountable and vulnerable.
- know how to listen to others and hear others' hearts.
- have learned how to grow through their own failures, knowing how to experience success in moving from one failure to the next without losing enthusiasm.
- are genuinely humble people.

I have known pastors who, out of pride, would not admit they needed help. As a result, the churches they led were limited by the problems in the lives of these men—not least of all by their lack of humility.

Jesus tells us the parable of someone who manages other servants and makes it clear that if this manager cares well for his subordinates, he will be well rewarded, but if he treats them badly, he will pay severely by being sent where unbelievers go (Luke 12:42-46). This seems to have a clear application to leaders and those who serve under them. We deduce that heaven will not be the final destination of leaders if they treat their flock badly.

Jesus told Wendy Alec that leaders need to be especially aware of pride because they too could fall, just as Satan did.[4] To become leaders, they have learned much and become proficient, and it must be tempting to take pride in the fact that in these areas they are different, and possibly better than the rest of us.

As one who has often played keyboard and sometimes led worship or preached, I am well aware how easy it is to become proud in those roles. I have had to repent many times and know that I am not alone in this. Pride is one of the most common temptations of singers and musicians. I once heard a minister say, "My church is lucky to have me," and one can only wonder what proud thoughts were behind that statement. If we are to lead, we should seek to glorify God and not preen ourselves.

Concern for status in the social or Christian community can lead to empire building instead of sharing resources with other churches or groups.

Pride in leaders may tempt them to assert undue control over others because

- they consider their own ideas better than those of others, and, therefore, those ideas should be implemented without question.

- they may not want any of their own ideas to be seen as inferior, and so rebuke, silence, or belittle anyone with conflicting or better ones.

Christian leaders are meant to be shepherds to their flock, but if these leaders assert undue control, they can become guilty of spiritual abuse. David Johnson and Jeff VanVonderen[5] have written an excellent book on this subject, concluding with some wisdom on the two options for those who are abused—fight or flight.

Individuals in a church may grow in faith beyond that of their minister, who at that point can feel threatened. The minister should not restrict the activities of such individuals, but encourage their involvement in church life wherever relevant—to the benefit of the whole church. It could mean giving them the "pulpit" occasionally.

Leaders may think that they know best, and they may be unwilling to listen to others or take advice. Because of this, they may not recognise when 'new ideas' from subordinates are actually the voice of the Holy Spirit. They probably do not realise when they are proud and may even resort to judgment and control, possibly by taking away privileges, opportunities, or responsibilities from individuals so that those individuals can no longer lead or serve in the way that God has equipped them.

If we are in leadership and proud, we know what to do—repent and humble ourselves. If, however, we recognise pride in leaders above us, the very nature of the problem is that they are unwilling to believe us if we point it out. The best course of action in these circumstances may be to pray and wait for God to intervene. He will often use circumstances to humble us or them when needed.

God's activities

It is God's desire that we are humble, so what does He do about it? For the Israelites, there was the wilderness experience that was designed to teach humility.

> Remember how the LORD your God led you all the way in the desert these forty years, to humble you and to test you in order to know what was in your heart, whether or not you would keep his commands. He humbled you, causing you to hunger and then feeding you with manna, which neither you nor your fathers had known, to teach you that man does not live on bread alone but on every word that comes from the mouth of the LORD. (Deut. 8:2-3)

We might question whether they needed this when they had been humbled by suppression in Egypt, but God knew what He was doing. What might happen today that could be compared to the wilderness experience? It could be that:

- nothing exciting happens
- we do not appear to be achieving much or anything at all

- we are not in a position to influence—just like Moses when he was a simple shepherd in the wilderness

Israelites in the wilderness were humbled, but later generations needed to learn the lesson also. We find that in the days of Jeremiah, God told them:

> To this day they have not humbled themselves or shown reverence, nor have they followed my law and the decrees I set before you and your fathers. 'Therefore, this is what the LORD Almighty, the God of Israel, says: I am determined to bring disaster on you and to destroy all Judah.' (Jer. 44:10-11)

On another occasion we find God dealing with pride when He gives Isaiah a prophecy about the downfall of Tyre. Isaiah says:

> The LORD Almighty planned it, to bring low the pride of all glory and to humble all who are renowned on the earth. (Isa. 23:9)

God might teach us to be humble by unseating us from a prominent position—as he did with Saul of Tarsus (knocked to the ground and no longer leading the persecution of Christians). Even Moses was taken out of the limelight after killing the Egyptian. Some modern equivalents could be:

- dropped from a leadership role
- no longer wanted in the worship group
- stopped from leading a home or cell group
- stopped from leading an alpha course

God may expose our sins, faults, and failings, and possibly apply gentle correction in our lives, as he did with Peter after the cock crowed (Luke 22:60-61). Alternatively, He may allow us to suffer adversity to bring us low as He did with Pharaoh. God had asked him via Moses:

> "'How long will you refuse to humble yourself before me? Let my people go, so that they may worship me. If you refuse to let them go, I will bring locusts into your country tomorrow.'" (Ex. 10:3-4)

Because Pharaoh still refused to humble himself before God, he was visited by a plague of locusts. From all these accounts, it is worth remembering that if God thinks people ought to be more humble, He is quite capable of either forcing circumstances on them to make them that way or removing protection so that they 'trip up' and fall.

God does not only discipline the proud, but He rewards the humble, as we can see from the following account. A book of the law was found in the temple and read to King Josiah, who, when he heard it, realised how angry God must be with the idolatry and other evil practices in the land. So, through a prophet, God told Josiah:

> "'Because your heart was responsive and you humbled yourself before God when you heard what he spoke against this place and its people, and because you humbled yourself before me and tore your robes and wept in my presence, I have heard you, declares the LORD. Now I will gather you to your fathers, and you will be buried in peace. Your eyes will not see all the disaster I am going

to bring on this place and on those who live
here.'" (2 Chron. 34:27-28)

For another example of how God might humble a person, we can read about his dealings with Nebuchadnezzar in Daniel 4, ending with the sentence, "And those who walk in pride he is able to humble."

Personal growth and progress

A long time before I began to study the subject of pride and humility, I thought I had conquered pride! I now know how wrong I was. In terms of Jesus's story of the plank and the speck, I now have a better idea how big a plank I had. I tried to remove specks from other people and made matters worse. I still grieve today for some of my past actions. As I have become more aware of my own pride, I realise how much I must strive to be humble.

Our enemy has an unlimited source of pride temptations to sow into our minds, which we must be vigilant to remove as soon as they occur. Many times I have had to repent and ask God's forgiveness for entertaining my pride for even a short while. I compiled the list of symptoms you have read earlier in the book to help me identify pride whenever it occurs, but I'm sure this list is not exhaustive, and you might like to add your own as they occur to you.

It is my hope, dear reader, that you have discovered whether pride exists in your life, and if so, what form it takes. It's a relatively simple matter to read about pride and humility, but to make full use of this information, we need the conviction and help from the Holy Spirit together with the persistence to play our part daily. I have seen how easy it is to learn a lesson academically without putting it into practice. Please do not fall into that trap.

This book has also been written so that we can all understand the importance of humility and the blessing it can bring. It could be a spiritual health warning for those who, until now, have largely ignored the pride in their lives. Each of us needs to realise how severely pride hinders our Christian progress and, furthermore, can even be the downfall of leaders who otherwise appeared to be in a strong position.

I find that I have to continue working at humility because occasions arise when it is so easy to be proud. It is my prayer that this little book will help Christians to eradicate the weeds of pride and cultivate the beautiful flowers of humility that delight the Lord. If we can achieve this, it will help His Church in many ways. It is my expectation that anyone who aims for humility will find joy and contentment also.

Even if we believe we are humble, there is further to go. Micah says, "And what does the LORD require of you? To act justly and to love mercy and to walk humbly with your God" (Micah 6:8). Let us soldier on!

Appendix 1:
Prayers for humility

Lord Jesus, take from me the longing for praise.
Lord, take from me the desire for respect, approval, and honour.

Lord, grant me the grace to desire that others may be pre-
ferred, praised, and consulted, when I am not.
Lord, grant me a teachable and obedient heart, that I may
learn your ways, and serve others joyfully.
Lord, grant me the strength of your Holy Spirit to be humble
and gentle like you.

Lord, deliver me from the fear of being lonely, forgotten, or
overlooked.
Lord, deliver me from the fear of being criticised, hurt, or
humiliated.
Lord, deliver me from the desire for comfort and ease.

Lord Jesus, help me to consider others more important than
myself, and cooperate with them to please you.

Appendix 2:
Biblical instructions to serve one another in love

Meeting

- Accept one another (Rom. 15:7)
- Greet one another with a holy kiss (Rom. 16:16)
- Have fellowship with one another (1 John 1:7)
- When you come together to eat, wait for one another (1 Cor. 11:33)

Harmony & unity

- Forgive whatever grievances you may have against one another (Col. 3:13)
- Encourage one another and build one another up (1 Thess. 5:11)
- Love one another (John 13:34)
- Be devoted to one another in brotherly love (Rom. 12:10)
- Have...concern for each other (1 Cor. 12:25)
- Be patient...(bearing with one another in love, Eph. 4:2)
- Pray for each other (James 5:16)
- Speak to one another (Eph. 5:19)

- Spur one another on toward love and good deeds (Heb. 10:24)
- Teach and admonish one another with all wisdom (Col. 3:16)

Personal regard

- Consider others better than yourselves (Phil. 2:3)
- Honour one another above yourselves (Rom. 12:10)
- Clothe yourselves with humility toward one another (1 Pet. 5:5)

Service

- Serve one another (Gal. 5:13)
- Wash one another's feet (John 13:14)
- Carry each other's burden (Gal. 6:2)
- Be kind and compassionate to one another (Eph. 4:32)
- Offer hospitality to one another without grumbling (1 Pet. 4:9)
- Each one should use whatever gift he has received to serve others (1 Pet. 4:10)

Further Reading

The Twelve Steps of Humility and Pride, **Bernard of Clairvaux**, Hodder and Stoughton Religious.

The Imitation of Christ, **Thomas** à Kempis, Dover Publications.

Humble is the Way, **David Jones**, McDougal & Associates.

Under Cover: The Promise of Protection Under His Authority, **John Bevere**, Thomas Nelson.

Living Below with the Saints We Know, **Brian Hathaway**, Eagle.

References

1   Taken from THE JESUS I NEVER KNEW (p118) by
    Philip Yancey. Copyright © 1995 by Philip Yancey. Use
    by permission of Zondervan. www.zondervan.com

2   **Rick Joyner**, *The Final Quest, p50-56*. Whitaker House.

3   **W.E. Vine, Merrill F. Unger and William White,** *Vine's
    complete expository dictionary of Old and New Testament
    words [computer file], electronic ed., Logos Library System,*
    (Nashville: Thomas Nelson) 1997, c1996.

4   **Wendy Alec,** *Journal of the Unknown Prophet, p266*.
    Warboys Media.

5   **David Johnson and Jeff VanVonderen**, *The Subtle
    Power of Spiritual Abuse*. Bethany House Publishers.